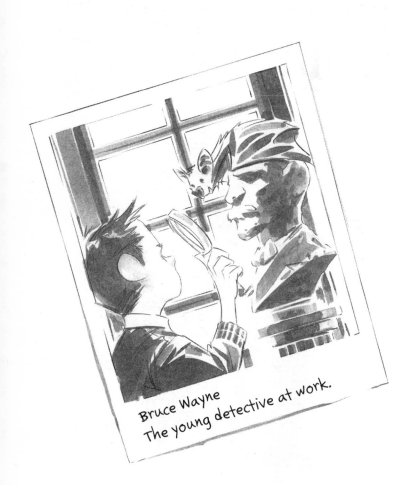

Bruce Wayne
The young detective at work.

DC COMICS
SECRET HERO SOCIETY

STUDY HALL OF JUSTICE

Written by **Derek Fridolfs** | Illustrations by **Dustin Nguyen**

SCHOLASTIC

To our editors; Rex, for helping launch us, and Michael, for seeing us through to the finish line.

To my teachers throughout the years who encouraged me to write inside and outside the margins. To my parents, for their constant love and support. And to Pamela, who listens to all my silly ideas with great enthusiasm. — Derek

Thanks to Mom, Phyllis, and my wife, Nicole, for always supporting my love for illustration, or at least putting up with it. — Dustin

SCHOLASTIC CHILDREN'S BOOKS
AN IMPRINT OF SCHOLASTIC LTD
EUSTON HOUSE, 24 EVERSHOLT STREET, LONDON, NW1 1DB, UK
REGISTERED OFFICE: WESTFIELD ROAD, SOUTHAM, WARWICKSHIRE, CV47 0RA
SCHOLASTIC AND ASSOCIATED LOGOS ARE TRADEMARKS AND/OR
REGISTERED TRADEMARKS OF SCHOLASTIC INC.

FIRST PUBLISHED IN THE UK BY SCHOLASTIC LTD, 2015

BOOK DESIGN BY RICK DEMONICO AND CHEUNG TAI

ISBN 978 1407 15714 6

A CIP CATALOGUE RECORD FOR THIS BOOK
IS AVAILABLE FROM THE BRITISH LIBRARY.

PRINTED BY CPI GROUP (UK) LTD, CROYDON, CR0 4YY
PAPERS USED BY SCHOLASTIC CHILDREN'S BOOKS ARE MADE
FROM WOOD GROWN IN SUSTAINABLE FORESTS.

1 3 5 7 9 10 8 6 4 2

WWW.SCHOLASTIC.CO.UK

August 3rd

Dear Mr. Wayne,

Congratulations! After reviewing your application, we have selected you as one of the lucky few to be accepted into our prestigious institution.

As one of our students, you will be taught by some of the finest professors and scientists. And you will learn alongside some of the most promising students of your age.

Many of our previous graduates have moved on to become captains of industry and to further our global cause of educational enlightenment. Your educational needs will be fulfilled with us.

We see great things in your future, Bruce, and I look forward to peeling back the layers of your mind.

Welcome to DUCARD.

Sincerely,

Professor Hugo Strange
School Admissions / Guidance Counselor

DATE: AUGUST 6

USERNAME: BWAYNE

RE: JOURNAL ENTRY 1

I JUST GOT MY ACCEPTANCE LETTER IN THE MAIL FOR THE DUCARD ACADEMY! ALFRED MADE ME WRITE SO MANY LETTERS TO EVERY SCHOOL THAT MY HAND ALMOST FELL OFF. BUT MY FIRST CHOICE ENDED UP BEING THE ONE I GOT, SO IT WAS A SUCCESS!

I CAN'T WAIT TO START AT MY NEW SCHOOL! NO MORE BORING TUTORS BROUGHT TO THE MANSION, OR ALFRED'S "ETIQUETTE" LESSONS. AND THE BEST PART—NO MORE CHORES! BUT ALFRED PROMISES ME MY CHORES WILL BE WAITING FOR ME WHEN I GET HOME FROM SCHOOL EACH DAY. *NOT FAIR!!*

I HOPE THE CAFETERIA FOOD IS AS GOOD AS ALFRED'S COOKING. DON'T TELL HIM I SAID THAT OR HE'LL ASK FOR A RAISE!

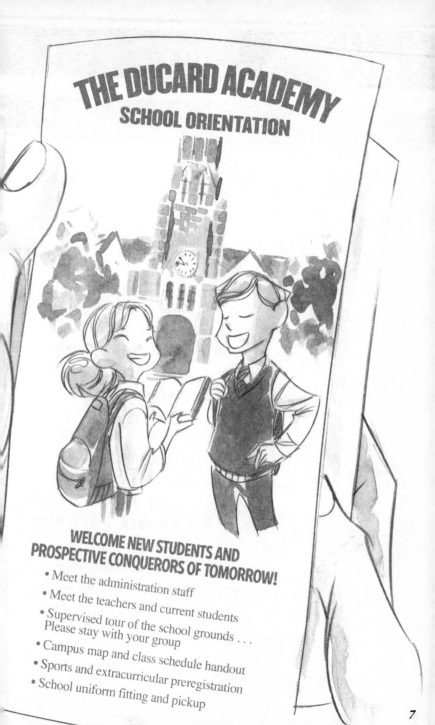

THE DUCARD ACADEMY
SCHOOL ORIENTATION

WELCOME NEW STUDENTS AND PROSPECTIVE CONQUERORS OF TOMORROW!

- Meet the administration staff
- Meet the teachers and current students
- Supervised tour of the school grounds . . . Please stay with your group
- Campus map and class schedule handout
- Sports and extracurricular preregistration
- School uniform fitting and pickup

ORIENTATION DAY

YOU ARE HERE FOR THE TOUR. I WILL SHOW YOU.

NOW. SINGLE FILE.

8

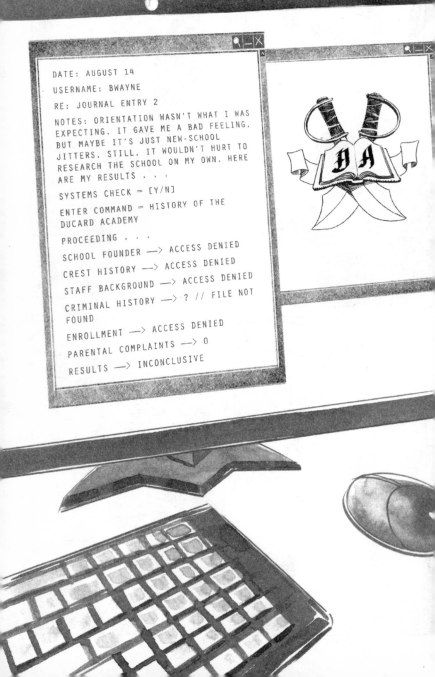

DATE: AUGUST 14
USERNAME: BWAYNE
RE: JOURNAL ENTRY 2
NOTES: ORIENTATION WASN'T WHAT I WAS
EXPECTING. IT GAVE ME A BAD FEELING.
BUT MAYBE IT'S JUST NEW-SCHOOL
JITTERS. STILL, IT WOULDN'T HURT TO
RESEARCH THE SCHOOL ON MY OWN. HERE
ARE MY RESULTS . . .

SYSTEMS CHECK = [Y/N]

ENTER COMMAND = HISTORY OF THE
DUCARD ACADEMY

PROCEEDING . . .

SCHOOL FOUNDER —> ACCESS DENIED

CREST HISTORY —> ACCESS DENIED

STAFF BACKGROUND —> ACCESS DENIED

CRIMINAL HISTORY —> ? // FILE NOT
FOUND

ENROLLMENT —> ACCESS DENIED

PARENTAL COMPLAINTS —> 0

RESULTS —> INCONCLUSIVE

HOW DO THE NEW STUDENTS LOOK?

THE RECRUITS?

"STUDENTS"! WE MUST KEEP UP APPEARANCES.

THEY ARE YOUNG. EAGER. MAYBE TOO EAGER.

THERE'S ONE . . . THE RICH KID . . . VERY NOSY. HE COULD BE TROUBLE FOR US.

I'LL BE SURE TO KEEP AN EYE ON HIM. I'VE ALREADY STARTED.

WHAT TO BRING . . .

- ❏ Enrollment letter
- ❏ Application
- ❏ Photo ID (Secret identities need not apply) *Wait—WHAT?!*
- ❏ Medical history
- ❏ Pen and paper
- ❏ Absolute loyalty *That's kinda weird.*

WHAT NOT TO BRING . . .

- ❏ Parents *Looks like you're staying home, Alfred.*
- ❏ Adults
- ❏ Authorities *Hmm . . .*

WHAT I NEED TO BRING (ALFRED'S SHOPPING LIST)

Infrared and night vision goggles

Military-grade stealth suit with grappling hook

Portable chem lab for analyzing microfragments and fingerprints

Computer with advanced facial recognition software

Pudding cups (chocolate peanut butter)

I am NOT buying you any of this! But I will buy you new underwear.
—Alfred

ALFRED, QUIT IT! EVERYONE IS STARING.

FORGETTING SOMETHING, MASTER BRUCE?

ALL THE MORE REASON TO LOOK PRESENTABLE.

YOU ARE A REFLECTION ON ME, EVEN IF YOU ARE GRUMPY.

I HAVE ALSO PREPARED YOUR LUNCH. GRANOLA . . . VERY HEALTHY.

16

17

DATE: SEPTEMBER 1

USERNAME: BWAYNE

RE: JOURNAL ENTRY 3

MY FIRST DAY AT SCHOOL WASN'T WHAT I WAS EXPECTING. IT'S SUPPOSED TO BE THE BEST ACADEMY FOR LEARNING IN GOTHAM CITY. BUT THE ONLY THING I LEARNED IS THAT NO SCHOOL IS PERFECT.

AM I JUST LOOKING FOR THE WORST, LIKE ALFRED SAYS?

ALFRED THINKS I'M A SCARED LITTLE BOY WHO NEEDS TO LEARN TO FOLLOW THE RULES. BUT I MUST GET TO THE BOTTOM OF WHAT'S GOING ON AT DUCARD.

HI!

YOU CAN SIT WITH US, IF YOU WANT.

WAS IT SOMETHING I SAID?

THE FACULTY

PRINCIPAL

PROFESSOR HUGO STRANGE
(School Admissions / Guidance Counselor)

DR. THADDEUS B. SIVANA
(Science)

MR. VANDAL SAVAGE
(History)

MR. JERVIS TETCH
(Literature)

MR. BASIL KARLO
(Theater/Arts)

MS. SIOBHAN McDOUGAL
(Choir)

COACH ZOD
(Boys' Physical Ed.)

COACH "KITTY" FAULKNER
(Girls' Physical Ed.)

MR. SOLOMON GRUNDY
(Homeroom)

HISTORY CLASS
"THE HISTORY OF MAN"
TEACHER—MR. VANDAL SAVAGE

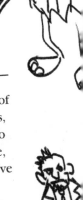

COURSE DESCRIPTION:

To examine the nature of humankind throughout history, from the dawn of civilization to the present.

COURSE OBJECTIVES:

To give an introduction to the origin and development of humankind throughout the ages. Our greatest successes, our failures, our inventions, discoveries, and impulses. To talk about human achievement in construction, science, technology, military, and politics. To discuss where we've been as a species and where we're going. These and other topics will provide lectures and group discussion, and be examined through quizzes and testing.

drawings elicit a positive response by teacher, who is made fun of.
useful evidence to keep a file on him

THE REST OF YOU WILL LEARN HISTORY. BUT THIS CLASS CLOWN *IS* HISTORY.

REPORT TO DETENTION.

HISTORY 101

All great empires reach a pinnacle of distinction and achievement before their inevitable destruction. Some due to the rise in power of their enemies. Some due to their own shortcomings. History is built on the rise and fall of these great empires and civilizations. But everything you've read is what they've chosen to tell you. And it has been wrong. No matter how bright the success, it is the shadows cast from their brilliance that are there to direct the course of the future.

What does this hold for your future?

Look to the Shadows ...

DATE: SEPTEMBER 4

USERNAME: BWAYNE

RE: JOURNAL ENTRY 4

THIS SCHOOL IS WEIRD!

YESTERDAY I FELT A KID BLUR PAST ME. TODAY I
WITNESSED A GIRL FLYING THROUGH THE AIR. I'M NOT
KIDDING. NOT TO MENTION THERE'S A TON OF CLOWNS
AND . . . I THINK I'VE EVEN SEEN NINJA LURKING
ABOUT.

IT'S CRAZY.

MY MIND AND BODY HAVE BEEN TRAINED BY THE VERY
BEST (ALFRED SAW TO THAT WITH PRIVATE TUTORS).
MY EYES AREN'T PLAYING TRICKS. SO THERE MUST BE
A LOGICAL EXPLANATION FOR IT.

MY INVESTIGATION CONTINUES. BUT I MUST ALSO MAKE
TIME TO BEAT LEVEL SEVEN OF **VIGILANTE FIGHTER
TURBO**. RESIST THE URGE TO DOWNLOAD A CHEAT CODE.

SEPTEMBER 5 . . .

HIGH IQ'S ONLY! YOU DON'T BELONG.

GET LOST!

YOOO-HOOO . . . OVER HERE. JOIN US FOR A LAUGH, BRUCIE!

31

SCHOOL IS FILLED WITH ALL KINDS OF KIDS. NERDS, JOCKS, CHEERLEADERS, AND CLASS CLOWNS. THEY'RE HARD TO AVOID.

I HAVE STARTED TO EAT IN THE LIBRARY INSTEAD AND MET OTHERS LIKE ME. CLARK IS A FARM KID FROM SMALLVILLE. DIANA IS AN EXCHANGE STUDENT FROM ACROSS THE SEA. THEY BOTH LIVE IN THE DORMS, AND THEY'RE IN MY HOMEROOM, TOO.

AT FIRST I THOUGHT THEY WERE ANNOYING. BUT THEY'RE AS CONFUSED AS I AM ABOUT SCHOOL. THEY ALSO WERE EXCITED ABOUT COMING HERE UNTIL THEY HAD THE SAME PROBLEMS.

MAYBE I DON'T HAVE TO INVESTIGATE THIS SCHOOL ALONE. MAYBE WE CAN DO IT TOGETHER. IT'S SOMETHING WORTH CONSIDERING.

SEPTEMBER 8—FIELD NOTES

It's the start of my second week at DUCARD and my experience hasn't improved.

Theater class this morning with Mr. Basil Karlo was weird. His room was filled with nothing but old posters of the movies he's been in. I think playing a "teacher" is his current act, because he stole a kid's backpack right in front of him—as part of the lesson! He told us to act like the people we want to become and take what we want. What kind of a class is this?!

Also I think he was sweating mud. SERIOUSLY!! I managed to take a sample of the claylike substance. Will run tests on it later. This school . . . this world . . . is bigger and weirder than I thought.

SCHOOL ANNOUNCEMENTS

- **Boys' sports:**
  All pain, some gain!
  To sign up, see Coach Zod

- **Cheer squad tryouts**
  Friday, October 10 at 3:00 p.m. after school
  in the girls' gymnasium

- **JOIN the bird-watchers society!**
  If interested, see club president
  Oswald Cobblepot.

- **NEED a tutor?** ←THeN yer a jerk!! hee-hee!
  Inspired by world domination?
  Evil geniuses wanted.

DIANA'S DIARY
SEPTEMBER 10

Ever since that weird computer talked to us in the library, I've been on edge. Bruce is right! There are a lot of strange things happening around here. It's a shame because this school seemed so promising in their invite letter. I was so excited to enroll and now all I am is mad. I've broken six pencils trying to write it all down.

Like, I just got out of literature class, and I'm starting to notice more things. Our teacher, Mr. Tetch, is forcing us to read only one book in class: Alice's Adventures in Wonderland. I mean, that book's okay. But the only one we're going to read? And that's not the only weird thing. He keeps a pet bunny that hops around the classroom. He calls every girl Alice (EVEN ME)! And he dresses just like the Mad Hatter. He gives me the creeps!

SCHOOL NURSE INCIDENT REPORT

STUDENT: Clark Kent

TEACHER: Ms. Siobhan McDougal

CLASS: Choir

DATE: September 10

DESCRIPTION OF THE INCIDENT:

Choir class today was described as being extra rowdy. When Ms. McDougal couldn't get control over her students, it was reported that she screamed. The volume of her voice was so loud, it broke the windows, and many students' ears were ringing.

ACTION TAKEN:

Most students were administered cotton and gauze to prevent swelling and provide protection. Any who felt dizzy were sent home.

FURTHER RECOMMENDED CARE:

None. Clark is one of the few that appears unaffected. He seems to have exhibited extraordinary hearing and durability. No further action is to be taken.

NOTES:

He possesses remarkable strength for his age. Perhaps he is extraordinary in other ways, too.

IF YOU HAVE ANY QUESTIONS ABOUT THIS EVENT, PLEASE CALL THE NURSE'S OFFICE.

39

DUE TO THE KANDOR VIRUS

THE SCHOOL LIBRARY WILL BE CLOSED
ON FRIDAY, SEPTEMBER 12,
FOR COMPUTER MAINTENANCE,
NETWORK RECONFIGURATION, AND
THE RECOVERY OF LOST DATA.

BRAINIAC IS SORRY
FOR THIS INCONVENIENCE
AND VOWS REVENGE.

GROUP CHAT

 bruce, clark—where are you?

 running a little late start without me.

 can't. the library is closed.

i know. cool, right?

 ?

i put BRAINIAC on sleep mode but the door locks are computerized with a rotating algorithm, too risky to break in.

 BREAK IN?!

 cool it, CK. bruce what do you want to talk about?

this school has been investigating us . . . HARD! invasive database searches, access to private documents, satellite scanning, maybe even wiretapping, and I still don't know for what reason.

 paranoid much? what proof do you have?

krypton, themyscira, BRAINIAC seemed to have those keywords on file concerning you guys. until i purged his system.

 what's a krypton? not me. i have no idea how. i swear. right guys? i mean i've never even come from that whatever it is

 CK, take a breath. bruce, what about u?

GROUP CHAT

doesn't matter, look i don't care about either of your secrets, only why they're so interested in us. do you need any more reason to join me?

no I'm in.

same here.

good. consider this your formal invite to my house this weekend. we'll go over the specifics of what our next move is. until then i've prepared some documents for you to read and study beforehand. i put them in each of your lockers.

i never gave you my locker combination.

CK

wha?

it's bruce. i'm sure he's figured out everyone's combination.

even the ones in the faculty lounge.

BRUCE!!!

anyways we'll discuss more at my house.

the faculty lounge is OFF-LIMITS.

that was a joke.

why do i not believe you?

also bring an appetite. alfred likes to cook, it's kinda his job.

SEND

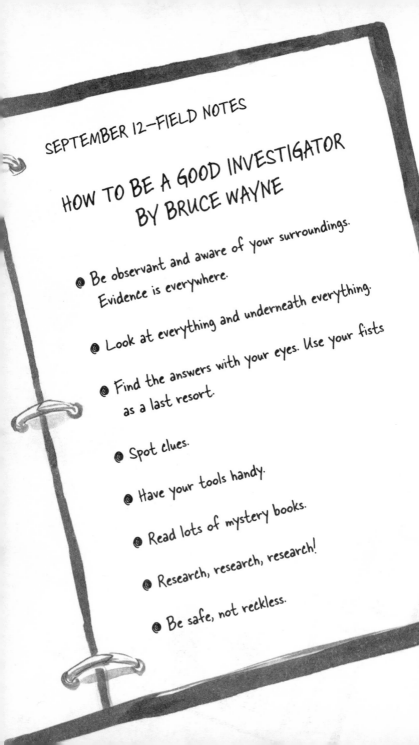

SEPTEMBER 12—FIELD NOTES

HOW TO BE A GOOD INVESTIGATOR BY BRUCE WAYNE

- Be observant and aware of your surroundings. Evidence is everywhere.

- Look at everything and underneath everything.

- Find the answers with your eyes. Use your fists as a last resort.

- Spot clues.

- Have your tools handy.

- Read lots of mystery books.

- Research, research, research!

- Be safe, not reckless.

SECRET FACULTY LOUNGE

EAST WING
LOCKER COMBINATIONS

WEST PATHWAY

UNIT 7

UNIT 8

UNIT 9

UNIT 10

SEPTEMBER 30—FIELD NOTES

MISSION #1—INFILTRATION

Our priority is for each of us to infiltrate various sectors of school and report back our findings.

BRUCE: I will attempt to "make friends" as a way to get information.

CLARK: You've been tasked with becoming "hall monitor." From that position, you'll be able to view any suspicious activity without drawing any attention.

DIANA: Your task is to join the cheer squad. It can provide different clues and leads to check up on.

We'll meet back in the library at the end of school each day to report our findings.

CAFETERIA-MONITOR 02

12:51:05

LIBRARY-MONITOR 03

02:25:16

CAFETERIA-MONITOR 04

12:36:19

DATE: OCTOBER 1

USERNAME: BWAYNE

RE: JOURNAL ENTRY 6

SO I TRIED TO MAKE FRIENDS TODAY. THAT DIDN'T GO SO WELL.

FIRST I DEVELOPED A DISGUISE SO I WOULDN'T BE RECOGNIZED. I CREATED "MATCHES MALONE," A ROUGH KID FROM ACROSS THE TRACKS, WITH HELP FROM A COSTUME AND MAKEUP I FOUND IN THEATER CLASS. BUT MY DISGUISE WAS BLOWN WHEN THE DRAMA TEACHER ANNOUNCED IT TO THE SCHOOL. THE TEACHERS ARE JUST AS BAD AS THE STUDENTS!

THE JOCKS ONLY WANTED TO USE ME AS TARGET PRACTICE. EVERY BALL IN GYM HAS NOW HIT ME. WORSE, THEY DUMPED ME IN THE TRASH. BANE EVEN TRIED TO PUT ME IN A WRESTLING HOLD, BUT I MANAGED TO GET AWAY.

THE NERDS HAD ALREADY MADE UP THEIR MINDS THAT I WASN'T SMART ENOUGH FOR THEM. THEY SHOWED ME EVERY REPORT CARD I'VE EVER GOTTEN AND EVERY TEST SCORE I'VE RECEIVED, AND LAUGHED AT ME. HOW DO THEY HAVE ACCESS TO THAT?! BESIDES, EVERYONE KNOWS I'M A GENIUS. IT'S JUST A FACT.

THE CLOWNS WERE THE ONLY ONES WILLING TO GIVE ME A SHOT. BUT THE JOKE WAS ENTIRELY ON ME, SINCE THEY SET ME UP. THE FOOD FIGHT I WAS ASKED TO START WAS TURNED AROUND ON ME AND THE ENTIRE SCHOOL JOINED IN . . . EVEN THE LUNCH LADY. I STILL SMELL LIKE FRENCH FRIES.

BEING REJECTED BY EVERYONE IS DEPRESSING. BUT I HAVE TO REMEMBER NOT TO TAKE IT PERSONALLY. I REALLY DON'T WANT ANY OF THESE STUDENTS AS MY FRIENDS. I'M ONLY DOING IT TO GET INFORMATION.

52

HALLWAY-MONITOR 03   10:15:11

FLOOR-MONITOR 01   10:15:15

HALLWAY-MONITOR 02   10:15:48

OFFICE-MONITOR 01   10:16:34

HALLWAY-MONITOR 01   10:16:51

53

HALL MONITOR—INCIDENT REPORT

STUDENT: _____ JOE KERR

DATE: __OCTOBER 7

LOCATION: ___ BOYS' BATHROOM / HALL

INCIDENT:

Subject was caught with friends trying to prank another
student with a bucket of water. He was apprehended
before he could finish the act.

ADDITIONAL NOTES:

This student and his friends have repeatedly been found
without hall passes, have been caught loitering, and
committing general acts of delinquency.

MONITOR ON DUTY: _____ CLARK KENT

Report never got a response and was dismissed.
I fished it from the office trash to keep on file for
my own records. —B

DUCARD ACADEMY
CHEER SQUAD TRYOUTS

Cheer your team to battle!
Chant your battle cry!
Conquer your enemies!
Dance in their defeat!

FRIDAY, OCTOBER 10–3:00 p.m.
Grass field behind the girls' gymnasium

DATE: OCTOBER 10

USERNAME: BWAYNE

RE: JOURNAL ENTRY 7

I'M DISAPPOINTED THAT OUR FIRST MISSIONS HAVE
BEEN A DISASTER.

AS HALL MONITOR, CLARK SPENT MORE TIME WRITING
REPORTS THAN FINDING OUT ANYTHING USEFUL. SO
I TOLD HIM TO JOIN THE SCHOOL NEWSPAPER. THAT
WAY HE CAN WRITE AS MUCH AS HE WANTS AND EXPOSE
ANYTHING ODD.

DIANA DIDN'T DO SO HOT, EITHER. SHE DIDN'T FIT
IN WITH THE GIRLS ON THE CHEER SQUAD, THEY
VIEWED HER AS AN OUTSIDER. AND WORSE . . . NOT
COOL.

I SUGGESTED HER NEXT MISSION COULD BE ONE OF
DIPLOMACY. BUT SHE GROWLED AT ME AND SAID SHE'D
TAKE ATHLETICS INSTEAD. PUNCHING MY LOCKER WAS
HER WAY OF ENDING OUR TALK DIPLOMATICALLY.

I WILL KEEP FINDING OTHER WAYS TO INVESTIGATE,
BUT FIRST I HAVE A "MANDATORY ASSESSMENT"
MEETING WITH THE GUIDANCE COUNSELOR. THIS MIGHT
COME IN HANDY, SINCE PROFESSOR HUGO STRANGE
EVALUATES ALL STUDENTS AT DUCARD.

STUDENT EVALUATION REPORT

STUDENT: __Bruce Wayne__   PROFESSOR: __Hugo Strange__

Which of the following best describes you?
Choose only one:

❏ Ambitious ❏ Angry ❏ Bored ❏ Calm ❏ Confused ❏ Creative ❏ Embarrassed
❏ Excited ☒ Focused ❏ Happy ❏ Hungry ❏ Lonely ❏ Loved ❏ Patient
❏ Proud ❏ Relieved ❏ Sad ❏ Scared ❏ Surprised ❏ Tired ❏ Other

Please rate the following based on how you are feeling about each area
of your life:

Friendships
Terrible
Great

1   2   3   4   ⑤   6   7   8   9   10

Home/Family
Terrible
Great

1   2   3   4   ⑤   6   7   8   9   10

Grades/School
Terrible
Great

1   2   3   4   ⑤   6   7   8   9   10

Diagnosis:

My assessment is that Bruce lives a very private life. Not willing to open
up or give clues to what he's thinking. He answered all my questions very
carefully and precisely. Not wavering one way or the other. While most
students struggle to find the path to who they are, I have a feeling Bruce
already knows what he wants. And that can be a dangerous thing.

Special Notes:

I hesitate to answer if Bruce is a worthy candidate for Nanda Parbat.
I will continue to keep a close eye on him before making a final
determination.

I was able to infiltrate and make a copy of this for
my own files without being noticed. The following is
security cam footage from before I deleted it from
the school system.

What is "Nanda Parbat"? This name requires further
investigating.   —B

THE DUCARD DAILY

OCTOBER 13

SCHOOL NEWSPAPER STAFF

VICTOR FRIES/WEATHER

"Freeze", reports the latest cold snap

CIRCE/HOROSCOPE

Bringing your weekly dose of horror

PAMELA ISLEY/
STAFF ENVIRONMENTAL REPORTER

Nature is nurture

65

THE DUCARD DAILY

OCTOBER 15

WEATHER REPORT
Victor Fries / Meteorologist

Cloudy 42°

Wind: 20 MPH

Chance of snow: Extremely likely

Fries's 5-Day Forecast: Rain, sleet, snow, snow, snow

PLANTS ARE BETTER THAN PEOPLE

Pamela Isley /
Staff Environmental Reporter
see page 4

HORROR SCOPES
by **Circe**

Cloudy days are ahead . . . rejoice! Every goal is within your grasp for the taking. Set your ideas into motion. Don't wait for the storm to pass . . . BE the storm! Seize the day by force. And if anyone tries to stop you, just tell them you get to do whatever you want.

UP, UP, AND AWAY!
by **Clark Kent** / Staff Reporter

As the newest journalist, I'd like to take this time to introduce myself. Growing up in Smallville, I learned many valuable lessons that would (continued on pg Z17)

AT THE PRINCIPAL'S OFFICE . . .

HI. IS THE PRINCIPAL AVAILABLE?

WHO ARE YOU?

CLARK KENT. THE NEW STAFF REPORTER.

YOU MIGHT'VE HEARD OF ME. MY LATEST ARTICLE MADE THE BACK PAGE. *WAAAY* IN THE BACK.

NO.

THE PRINCIPAL ONLY MEETS WITH THOSE HE DEEMS WORTHY. NO PRESS!

YOU CAN ONLY BE IN THE OFFICE IF YOU HAVE A SCHEDULED APPOINTMENT OR IF YOU'RE THE CLASS PRESIDENT. OTHERWISE . . . SCRAM!

HMM . . . *CLASS PRESIDENT!*

GIRLS' SPORTS SYLLABUS

Physical Fitness and Obedience Rules
by
COACH "KITTY" FAULKNER

THE DOS AND DON'TS TO PULVERIZE
YOUR OPPONENT:

- DO fight
- DO cheat
- DO steal

- DON'T play fair
- DON'T be a good sport

*GIVE OUT DISCIPLINE OR BE
DISCIPLINED!!!*

69

70

STUDENT EVALUATION REPORT

STUDENT: Diana Prince   **PROFESSOR:** Hugo Strange

Which of the following best describes you?
Choose only one:

❏ Ambitious ☒ Angry ❏ Bored ❏ Calm ❏ Confused ❏ Creative ❏ Embarrassed
❏ Excited ❏ Focused ❏ Happy ❏ Hungry ❏ Lonely ❏ Loved ❏ Patient
❏ Proud ❏ Relieved ❏ Sad ❏ Scared ❏ Surprised ❏ Tired ❏ Other

Please rate the following based on how you are feeling about each area
of your life:

Friendships
Terrible
Great

| 1 | 2 | ③ | 4 | 5 | 6 | 7 | 8 | 9 | 10 |

Home/Family
Terrible
Great

| 1 | 2 | 3 | 4 | 5 | 6 | ⑦ | 8 | 9 | 10 |

Grades/School
Terrible
Great

| 1 | 2 | 3 | ④ | 5 | 6 | 7 | 8 | 9 | 10 |

Diagnosis:

As a foreign exchange student, Diana struggles to fit in and belong. This
may be due to a sheltered upbringing or royal heritage. She holds herself
to a higher standard and falls short. Her weakness is her unwavering
nobility and fairness. But her strength is her quick-tempered anger,
which we can greatly exploit.

Special Notes:

She is a strong possibility for Nanda Parbat, but must be pushed further
for us to be absolutely certain.

That name again, "Nanda Parbat." This can't be a
coincidence. High priority to find out what it means!

—B

DATE: OCTOBER 20
USERNAME: BWAYNE
RE: JOURNAL ENTRY 8

OUR SECOND MISSIONS WEREN'T ANY BETTER.

CLARK JOINED THE SCHOOL NEWSPAPER. BUT ANYTHING
HE WRITES GETS MOVED TO THE LAST PAGE. MOST ISN'T
EVEN PRINTED. THEY SEEM TO ONLY WRITE ABOUT
MEAN THINGS AND WEIRDNESS. AND HE'S TOO NICE TO
REALIZE HE'S WASTING HIS TIME.

BUT HE CAME UP WITH THE IDEA OF RUNNING FOR CLASS
PRESIDENT. NOT A BAD IDEA! IT'LL ALLOW HIM ACCESS
TO THE SCHOOL OFFICE IF HE WINS.

DIANA WAS CUT FROM THE ATHLETICS TEAM. SHE WAS SO
MAD THAT I COULD HEAR HER YELLING ACROSS CAMPUS.
I ADMIRE HER DETERMINATION, BUT NOT HER TEMPER.

I'VE DECIDED TO MAKE HER CLARK'S CAMPAIGN
MANAGER. THAT WAY, SHE CAN FOCUS ON GETTING THE
FARM BOY ELECTED.

I'M STILL INVESTIGATING THE PHRASE "NANDA
PARBAT." SO FAR I'M HITTING DEAD ENDS, BUT IT'S
THE ONLY LEAD I HAVE.

ENTER SEARCH COMMAND > NANDA PARBAT

WARNING: SECURITY BREACH!!!
ENCRYPTION DETECTION = FAIL
ACCESS DENIED

WARNING: SECURITY BREACH!!!
ENCRYPTION DETECTION = FAIL
ACCESS DENIED

THE DUCARD DAILY

Okay, ghouls and goblins. Tomorrow's Halloween!

Time to ditch your school clothes and dress accordingly. Taunt, scare, and get into trouble . . . It's what you're supposed to do.

Don't smash any pumpkins, or face my wrath!!!

— **Pamela Isley**/Staff Environmental Reporter

GROUP CHAT

 u sound kinda paranoid.

 bruce sounds like bruce. xp

. . . i think we need to develop secret identities.

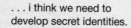 because that worked so well for you last time, "matches malone." ;)

. . . just mask up in costume for halloween tomorrow.

do it.

 ok.

 ttyl

SEND

FINE! THEN WHAT ARE YOU BOTH SUPPOSED TO BE?

WHAT DOES THE "S" STAND FOR?

OH, IT'S FROM MY HOME PLANET . . . ER, I MEAN HOMETOWN . . . YEAH, "S" IS FOR SMALLVILLE.

I LIKE IT!

HE STILL LOOKS THE SAME, EVEN WITHOUT GLASSES. WHERE'S THE MASK?

I AM AN AMAZON WARRIOR!

YOU LOOK WONDERFUL.

YOU'RE NOT WEARING A MASK, EITHER?

≥GRUMBLE . . .≤

TIRED OF WORKING ALONE TO
RULE THE WORLD?

SEEKING INJUSTICE IN
A JUST SOCIETY?

LET'S GANG TOGETHER AND
COME UP WITH THE SOLUTION!

[
MEET IN THE LIBRARY AFTER SCHOOL
AND COMBINE OUR BRAINPOWER.
]

DATE: NOVEMBER 1

USERNAME: BWAYNE

RE: JOURNAL ENTRY 9

HALLOWEEN REVEALED A LOT TO ME.

THE STUDENTS REALLY LIKED DRESSING UP. NOT
BECAUSE OF THE HOLIDAY. BUT TO GET INTO TROUBLE.
THEY SHOWED THEIR TRUE COLORS.

MY FRIENDS' COSTUMES NEED WORK. THEY NEED MASKS!
OTHERWISE, EVERYONE WILL RECOGNIZE THEM. BUT AT
LEAST THEY'RE PLAYING ALONG.

WHO IS CLARK KENT, REALLY? HE'S MORE THAN A FARM
KID. BUT HE'S TOO GOOD TO LIE. WHAT'S HE HIDING?

AND DIANA HAS SOMETHING ELSE GOING ON, TOO.
SHE'S STRONGER THAN EVERYONE ELSE. AND THAT
CROWN SHE WEARS LOOKS ROYAL. WHAT ISLAND IS SHE
FROM?

HOW WILL I FIND TIME TO INVESTIGATE THE SCHOOL
AND MY FRIENDS?

HALLWAY-MONITOR 04

15:21:14

HALLWAY-MONITOR 03

15:22:02

HALLWAY-MONITOR 04

15:22:46

HALLWAY-MONITOR 04

15:23:12

THE DUCARD DAILY

NOVEMBER 4

CLARK KENT
VS.
LEX LUTHOR
PRESIDENTIAL DEBATE TOMORROW!

WEATHER REPORT
Victor Fries/Meteorologist

Overcast 30°

Wind: 10 MPH

Fries's 5-Day Forecast: Frosty

HORROR SCOPES
by **Circe**

The future looks bright . . .
Don't let it be. Don't listen
to others. Your vote is all that
matters. Be your own leader.
And remember, it's what's on
the outside that counts!

Cast your vote with your voice instead of a ballot. Save a tree!!!!!

— **Pamela Isley**/Staff Environmental Reporter

DATE: NOVEMBER 4

USERNAME: BWAYNE

RE: JOURNAL ENTRY 10

CLARK CONTINUES TO STRUGGLE PRESENTING HIMSELF
AS THE BEST OPTION FOR CLASS PRESIDENT.
IT DIDN'T TAKE MUCH TO UPSET HIM. WHAT I DIDN'T
EXPECT WAS HOW HE'D REACT.

LASER-BEAM EYES? FURTHER FUELING MY SUSPICIONS
THAT CLARK IS NOT WHO OR WHAT HE APPEARS TO BE.

AT LEAST HE'S ON OUR SIDE. IF NOT, I'LL HAVE
TO FIND OUT HIS WEAKNESS. MINE IS CHOCOLATE CHIP
COOKIES. (ALFRED—IF YOU'RE READING THIS . . .
TAKE ADVANTAGE OF MY WEAKNESS!)

SPEECH LIST

Tell the truth.

Don't be afraid to avoid questions.

Present what you stand for.

Say what they want to hear.

Emphasize your best qualities.

Don't be snobby.

Just be yourself.

Be who they want you to be.

They want you to be more like THEM. Play along.

Photos—Ducard Presidential Debate

Our candidates take the stage.

"I'm a farm boy from Smallville, I wanna do good things."

"Good things? Boring . . ."

Lex knows what the crowd wants.

"Lex! Lex! Lex!"

Lex made Clarky cry.

Campaign advisor Diana clearly
telling him to vote Lex!

His own team agrees.
VOTE LEX!

The farm boy claims Lex is a cheater
and has proof. Yeaaaaah, riiiiight.

REPORT CARD

STUDENT: Lex Luthor   **HOMEROOM:**

LEVEL: **SEMESTER:**

Subject	Grade	Teacher Notes
ENGLISH	A+++	Now you're speaking my language $$$ Thx!
MATH	A+++	Computer hacking shows initiative. Well done!
SCIENCE	A++++	I gave you one extra plus. Or maybe you did? Quite the mad scientist!
ART	A+++	Thanks for your generous donation to me. You passed with flying colors.
HISTORY	A+++	You've learned the greatest historical lesson: *Money is power.*

99

STUDENT EVALUATION REPORT

STUDENT: __Clark Kent__   PROFESSOR: __Hugo Strange__

Which of the following best describes you?
Choose only one:

☒ Ambitious ☐ Angry ☐ Bored ☐ Calm ☐ Confused ☐ Creative ☐ Embarrassed
☐ Excited ☐ Focused ☐ Happy ☐ Hungry ☐ Lonely ☐ Loved ☐ Patient
☐ Proud ☐ Relieved ☐ Sad ☐ Scared ☐ Surprised ☐ Tired ☐ Other

Please rate the following based on how you are feeling about each area
of your life:

Friendships
Terrible   Great
1   2   ③   4   5   6   7   8   9   10

Home/Family
Terrible   Great
1   2   3   4   5   6   7   8   9   ⑩

Grades/School
Terrible   Great
1   2   3   4   5   6   ⑦   8   9   10

Diagnosis:

Clark is eager to please others. To be the best and rise above everyone, to
be a great role model. But is that what we're looking for? No one is perfect.
Everyone has some weakness. But so far, no one has been able to find any.
Losing the election should've knocked him down a notch.
But he seems as upbeat as ever. It's troubling.

Special Notes:

His power can help our cause or hurt us. If we can't work with him, then
we must work against him.

This confirms my suspicions that Clark is of alien origin.
If they're afraid of him, that has to be a good thing,
as long as he stays on the side of good.   —B—B

LATER, AT LUNCH . . .

HEY, LOOK . . . APPLESAUCE! ENOUGH HERE FOR EVERYONE.

YOU PLAYED RIGHT INTO LEX'S HANDS, WHICH IS WHY YOU LOST. YOU DIDN'T EVEN TRY TO BEND YOUR SPEECH OR PLATFORM TO FIT THE REST OF THE SCHOOL.

I CAN'T BE ANYONE BUT MYSELF.

I FIND THAT HARD TO BELIEVE, ALIEN.

WHAT?!

SMASH!

DATE: NOVEMBER 15

USERNAME: BWAYNE

RE: JOURNAL ENTRY 11

I KNOW NOW THAT EVERYONE WAS BROUGHT TOGETHER FOR A REASON. THAT MUCH IS FOR CERTAIN. BUT FIGURING THIS OUT HAS CAUSED TROUBLE.

TODAY I CLOSED OUR CRIMINAL INVESTIGATION UNIT. IT WASN'T WORKING. EACH OF US HAS OUR OWN SECRETS. AND WORKING TOGETHER IS NO LONGER A PRIORITY.

I WAS HOPING FOR PARTNERS, FELLOW INVESTIGATORS, EVEN FRIENDS. BUT I FEAR I HAVE NONE OF THOSE ANYMORE.

MAYBE IT'S FOR THE BEST. I'M BUMMED NOT TO HAVE SOMEONE TO HANG OUT WITH AND TALK STRATEGY . . . OR EVEN VIDEO GAMES. BUT I'LL JUST DO IT ALONE. I'M USED TO THAT.

I JUST NEED A NEW PLACE TO DO MY WORK. THE LIBRARY NO LONGER FEELS RIGHT.

NEW POSSIBLE LOCATIONS FOR SECRET HEADQUARTERS:

- RESTROOM (unfavorable odor and an accident waiting to happen)

- BASEBALL BACKSTOP (Selina and her gang of friends hang out there often)

- CAFETERIA DUMPSTER (pros: food access; cons: garbage)

- BEHIND THE MUSIC BUILDING (noise not conducive to my work)

- COMPUTER ROOM (access to information, but raises awareness)

- SCIENCE LAB (great for forensics, but Lex around too much)

Keep looking . . .

DATE: NOVEMBER 20

USERNAME: BWAYNE

RE: JOURNAL ENTRY 12

WITH THE LIBRARY ABANDONED AFTER DISBANDING THE
CRIMINAL INVESTIGATION UNIT, I HAVE DECIDED
UPON A NEW LOCATION TO CONTINUE MY WORK ALONE.
I'VE SELECTED THE JANITOR'S BASEMENT. LOCATED
UNDER THE SCHOOL AWAY FROM SPYING EYES, IT'S
THE PERFECT SPOT. CURRENTLY, IT IS USED AS A
STORAGE FACILITY FOR SCHOOL AND OFFICE SUPPLIES,
GARDENING EQUIPMENT, AND BATHROOM ITEMS. BUT NO
ONE EVER COMES DOWN HERE. IT'S AS SAFE A PLACE
AS ANY TO WORK FOR NOW.

Bruce cordially invites you to
Wayne Manor on November 27
to celebrate
Thanksgiving among
friends and family.

The following menu will be served:
- Butternut squash bisque
- Fall wedge salad
- Roast turkey breast with traditional mashed potatoes, cranberry sauce, giblet gravy, and Alfred's special sausage-sage stuffing
- Crustless pumpkin pie

Please RSVP if you are able to attend.

Thank you!

THANKSGIVING . . .

SCHOOL NURSE INCIDENT REPORT

STUDENT: Bryce Wayne
TEACHER: Coach Zod
CLASS: Boys' PE
DATE: December 1

DESCRIPTION OF THE INCIDENT:
There was a fight in class. Some students started wrestling with one another. Bruce appears to have a sore head. Clark Kent and Bane were also involved.

ACTION TAKEN:
Each student was examined and treated. Following that, Bruce was sent to detention. Clark spoke of a stomachache, but was not very convincing, and was also given detention.

FURTHER RECOMMENDED CARE:
None.

NOTES:
He possesses remarkable strength for his age. Perhaps he is extraordinary in other ways, too.

IF YOU HAVE ANY QUESTIONS ABOUT THIS EVENT, PLEASE CALL THE NURSE'S OFFICE.

Diana Prince
December 1

GIRLS' PHYSICAL EDUCATION—POP QUIZ
COACH "**KITTY**" FAULKNER Class of Hard Knocks

If someone steals money out of your locker during class, and you find out who did it, what do you do?

It is wrong to steal. And violence should be avoided.
There can always be more peaceful options. Confront
and talk to them. Work it out. You might end up
becoming friends.

OFFICE—INCIDENT REPORT

STUDENT: _____ DIANA PRINCE _____

DATE: _ DECEMBER 2 _____

LOCATION: ___ GIRLS' PE _____

INCIDENT:

Student is filing a complaint of cheating and
name-calling committed by the other students in
class. Also for the coach allowing it to happen.
When confronted, the coach said that when
competing against others, there's no such thing
as unfair. The student disagreed and was given
detention.

Found this filed away in the office while
investigating. It's good to read that Diana
continues even if we are no longer a team.
—B

117

118

DATE: DECEMBER 3

USERNAME: BWAYNE

RE: JOURNAL ENTRY 13

SO . . . I'M STUCK IN AFTER-SCHOOL DETENTION FOR
A WEEK. ALFRED IS DISAPPOINTED IN ME. I THINK
BECAUSE MY CHORES ARE NOW DELAYED. RIGHT?

DETENTION IS A WASTE OF TIME. BRAINIAC HAS GIVEN
US TASKS TO KEEP US BUSY. FILING PAPERWORK,
CATEGORIZING THE LIBRARY, RETURNING BOOKS,
AND SEEKING BACKGROUND INFORMATION ON OTHER
STUDENTS.

I NEED TO FIND A WAY OUT!!!

I DID MANAGE TO SNEAK IN A SMALL HIDDEN CAMERA
AND WAS ABLE TO TAKE PICTURES. I STILL SPOT
NINJA, BOTH AROUND CAMPUS AND NOW IN THE
LIBRARY. THEY ARE EVERYWHERE! MAYBE I NEED TO
TRACK THEM INSTEAD.

GLOOMBOOK

VIEW ACTIVITY LOG_FOE REQUESTS_MAIL
<GLOOMBOOK LOGIN PROTOCOL ACHIEVED>
<POKE REQUEST>

 HEY, YOU GUYS THERE?

 HERE

 WHAT DO YOU WANT?

 I KNOW YOU DON'T WANT TO TALK, BUT WE REALLY NEED TO.

 BRAINIAC HAS BEEN MAKING ME FILE PAPERWORK. BUT REALLY HE'S PROBING ME FOR INFORMATION ABOUT THE TWO OF YOU.

 HE ASKED ABOUT YOU AS WELL.

 YEAH. SO?

 WE HAVE TO GET OUT OF HERE. BUT TO DO SO, WE'LL HAVE TO WORK TOGETHER.

BECAUSE THAT WORKED SO WELL THE LAST TIME >:(

 IT BEATS BOOKKEEPING. SO WHAT'S THE PLAN?

 WE NEED TO DISTRACT HIM.

 WHAT GOOD IS THAT IF WE CAN'T GET OUT? REMEMBER THOSE DOORS ARE ELECTRONICALLY LOCKED AND CONTROLLED BY BRAINIAC.

 CAN WE SHUT OFF BRAINIAC? HE MUST HAVE AN OFF SWITCH.

 NOT WITHOUT DRAWING ATTENTION.

 SO WE'VE GOT NOTHING.

 FOR NOW. BUT TOMORROW WE CAN—

 YOU ARE UNAUTHORIZED TO BE HERE ACCESS DENIED

DATE: DECEMBER 4

USERNAME: BWAYNE

RE: JOURNAL ENTRY 14

IT'S NOT FUN, BUT I'M TEAMED UP WITH CLARK AND DIANA AGAIN. IT'S THE ONLY WAY WE CAN WORK TOWARD ESCAPING DETENTION.

SO FAR, WE'VE BEEN UNSUCCESSFUL. EVERY WAY OUT APPEARS TO BE BLOCKED BY BRAINIAC. HE ELECTRONICALLY LOCKS THE DOORS. THE ELECTRICAL MAINFRAME OF THE BUILDING RUNS THROUGH HIS SYSTEM. WE CAN'T ACCESS THE COMPUTERS IN THE LIBRARY. AND HE'S CONSTANTLY WATCHING EVERYTHING WE DO AND KEEPING US WORKING.

I BELIEVE I HAVE A PLAN TO GET US OUT. BUT IT REQUIRES A LITTLE MAPMAKING, SOME TIMING, AND A LOT OF LUCK. I'LL PRESENT IT TO THE OTHERS TOMORROW AND SEE WHAT THEY THINK.

Escape Plan!

123

DATE: DECEMBER 5

USERNAME: BWAYNE

RE: JOURNAL ENTRY 15

KNOWING HOW BAD BEHAVIOR IS REWARDED AT DUCARD,
WE'VE BEEN PRAISED AND LEFT ALONE AFTER OUR
SUCCESSFUL BREAKOUT FROM DETENTION.

I'VE DECIDED TO RE-FORM THE CRIMINAL
INVESTIGATION UNIT. HAVING PATCHED THINGS UP,
I'M HAPPY TO BE WITH MY FRIENDS AGAIN. EVEN
THOUGH I'M FULLY EQUIPPED TO WORK ALONE. I'M
JUST SAYING.

OUR NEW MISSION IS TO GO DIRECTLY TO THE TOP.
WHO IS THE MASTERMIND BEHIND THIS SCHOOL
AND WHAT IS THEIR ENDGAME? SOMEONE IS PULLING
EVERYONE'S STRINGS BUT DOES SO FROM THE SHADOWS.
IT'S TIME TO LURE THEM OUT AND SEE WHO THEY ARE.

DUCARD
HOLIDAY PROGRAM
DECEMBER 15
8:00 P.M.—DUCARD AUDITORIUM

'Tis the season . . .
Come join us for a little bit of holiday doom and gloom.
Our students are prepared to put on a program with
singing, dancing, and festive decorations.

Cookie and candy snacks will be provided to all your li'l
bad boys and girls after the concert.

Join us and help celebrate!

129

THE DUCARD DAILY

LETTER FROM THE PRESIDENT
by Lex Luthor

As winter break approaches, I wish all of you time off to rest and enjoy the coming of the new year. And for all your mad desires to be fulfilled. There's lots to conquer next year.

Let's get to it!

THERE'S NO DAY LIKE A SNOW DAY.
SEE YOU NEXT WINTER . . .

—Victor Fries

...wn with Alfred.

...pons trainin...
...h Artemis

Merry Christmas from Paradise!

new puppy!

made a
boom

...ner cool cave
...e east wing!

working on my ~~spaceship~~
tractor.

133

DATE: JANUARY 5

USERNAME: BWAYNE

RE: JOURNAL ENTRY 16

WINTER BREAK IS COMING TO AN END AND SCHOOL STARTS TOMORROW. WHILE OTHERS SPENT THEIR TIME WITH THEIR FAMILIES AND TRAVELING, I DECIDED TO STAY IN THE MANSION AND CONTINUE MY INVESTIGATIONS INTO THE SCHOOL. I ALSO FOUND TIME TO TRY OUT MY NEW SLED AND ALFRED'S SNOWMOBILE (BUT DON'T TELL HIM).

I'VE BEEN ABLE TO NARROW "NANDA PARBAT" AS A LOCATION. BUT NOT SPECIFICALLY WHERE. I'VE EXHAUSTED ALL MEANS ON MY COMPUTER. I MAY HAVE TO SEEK ALTERNATIVE MEANS I'VE NEVER CONSIDERED BEFORE . . . HIRING OUTSIDE HELP.

I'M HOPING THE REST OF THE SCHOOL YEAR WILL YIELD RESULTS MORE PROMISING THAN LAST YEAR. I CAN'T IMAGINE STAYING AT THIS SCHOOL FOR MUCH LONGER.

SCIENCE 101—LAB SYLLABUS
DR. THADDEUS B. SIVANA

If you are here to study the periodic table, do frog dissections, and discuss proven theories . . . then you are in the wrong class.

I shall expand your minds with the possibilities of all that is out there yet to be discovered and attempted. Only then can you become the mad scientist your dark desires have dreamt of.

- Create black holes

- Discover new uses for antimatter

- Absolve gravity

- Pioneer alternate dimensional time travel

- Unfold trans-warp technology

- Blot out the sun

GREETINGS, FUTURE SCIENTISTS OR LAB DISASTERS! I AM DR. SIVANA.

NOT EVERYONE WILL SURVIVE THIS CLASS. BUT THOSE THAT DO WILL BECOME THE GREAT MAD SCIENTISTS OF TOMORROW.

THOSE THAT DON'T . . . WELL . . .

YOU SHOULD ALL STRIVE TO BE THE BEST, LIKE LEX HERE.

HE SURVIVED A LAB EXPLOSION THAT TOOK AWAY HIS HAIR. IT TRANSFORMED HIM INTO A GREAT SCIENTIST.

FIRST ORDER OF BUSINESS IS YOU MUST DRESS THE PART.

EVERYONE GETS A WHITE LAB COAT AND DARK GLOVES.

YOU MUST ALSO BE ASSIGNED A PARTNER.

IT IS UP TO YOU TO DECIDE WHO WILL BE THE SCIENTIST AND WHO IS ONLY THE HENCHMAN—OR HENCHWOMAN, AS THE CASE MAY BE.

CAREER FAIR

Undecided about your future?
Unsure whether to rule the world or rule the galaxy?

This event is for you!
Learn about all kinds of different jobs! See the special clothes and uniforms they wear, participate in demonstrations, activities, and more!

Plus, free food and the chance to win great prizes!!

DATE: January 30
TIME: 1:00–3:00 p.m.
LOCATION: Ducard Auditorium

DATE: JANUARY 14
FROM: BWAYNE
TO: SMALLVILLE_KID, DIANA_WW41
SUBJECT: CAREER FAIR

A NEW FLYER HAS CAUGHT MY
ATTENTION. NOW THAT WE'RE ACTIVE
AGAIN, I THINK OUR NEW MISSION
SHOULD BE TO ATTEND THE CAREER
FAIR AT SCHOOL. LOOK FOR ANYTHING
SUSPICIOUS. AND TRY TO SPOT THE
PRINCIPAL.

—B

141

DATE: FEBRUARY 1

USERNAME: BWAYNE

RE: JOURNAL ENTRY 17

THIS "EVIL" CAREER FAIR DIDN'T PAN OUT TO
BE ANYTHING. IT FEATURED A LOT OF QUESTIONABLE
COMPANIES LOOKING FOR STUDENTS TO SHAPE
TO THEIR OWN BENEFIT. MOST SEEMED TO HAVE
WEIRD OPERATIONS RUNNING ON PRIVATE ISLANDS
OR ABANDONED MILITARY COMPOUNDS. THE ONLY ONE
THAT SHOWED ANY INTEREST IN ME WAS THE ARKHAM
FACILITY. I'LL HAVE TO REMEMBER TO FIND OUT
MORE ABOUT THEM.

AND IT WAS NO SURPRISE THAT THE PRINCIPAL
WAS NOWHERE TO BE FOUND. HOW DO YOU EVEN RUN
A SCHOOL IF YOU NEVER APPEAR AT THEIR
FUNCTIONS?

143

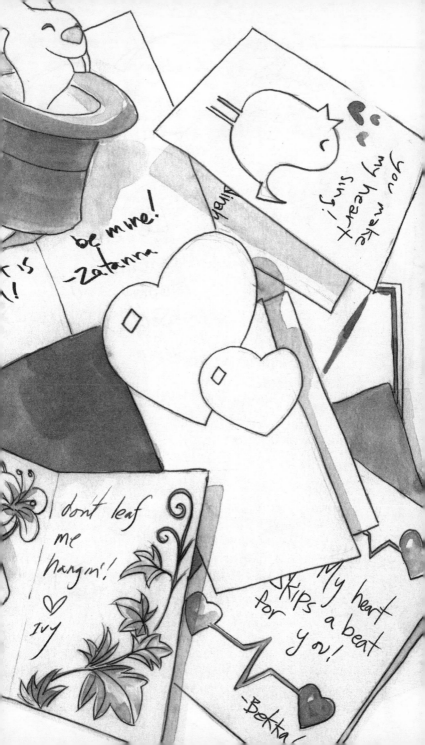

DATE: FEBRUARY 18

USERNAME: BWAYNE

RE: JOURNAL ENTRY 18

I HAVE DECIDED TO TAKE MATTERS INTO MY OWN
HANDS, BUT I NEED A COMPUTER TO DO IT. ALFRED
CONTINUES TO TAKE AWAY MY INTERNET PRIVILEGES
AT HOME FOR ANY NUMBER OF OFFENSES. THIS TIME
IT WAS FOR USING HIS PHONE TO ORDER PIZZA. HE
SEEMS TO THINK TWENTY OF THEM IS A LOT AND A
PUNISHABLE OFFENSE. BUT I WAS HUNGRY!

WITHOUT ACCESS TO MY HOME COMPUTER AND DENIED
ACCESS THROUGH THE SCHOOL, I HAVE DECIDED
TO TURN TO AN OUTSIDE CONSULTANT TO HELP ME
WITH MY SEARCH FOR "NANDA PARBAT." A PRIVATE
INVESTIGATION AGENCY I'M PAYING FOR OUT OF MY
BIRTHDAY AND HOLIDAY ALLOWANCE.

I AWAIT THEIR RESPONSE.

"If you're looking for an answer, then we've got the Question."

February 25

Wayne Manor of Gotham City
c/o Bruce Wayne
Re: Nanda Parbat

Dear Bruce,

I was able to uncover the answer to your inquiry about the name Nanda Parbat, but it wasn't easy. Not through normal records and background checks. More from anonymous sources and conspiracy channels off the beaten path. So without further ado . . .

Nanda Parbat is a fabled hidden city located in the mountains of Tibet. Its exact location and purpose is unknown. But it dates back many centuries.

I realize it's not much, but at least it's something. May the information be put to good use.

Sincerely,

VIC

Vic Sage, PI

DATE: MARCH 2
FROM: BWAYNE
TO: SMALLVILLE_KID, DIANA_WW41
SUBJECT: SUSPENSION

I'VE BEEN SUSPENDED FROM SCHOOL
FOR THE WEEK. THIS IS WHAT HAPPENS
WHEN YOU GET TOO CLOSE TO THE
TRUTH. THAT, AND NINJA JUMP YOU
(YES, I'M SERIOUS . . . NINJA!!!)

IT'S UP TO YOU BOTH TO KEEP
INVESTIGATING THE SCHOOL WHILE I'M
AWAY. THEN FILL ME IN ON WHAT YOU
FIND.

—B

153

Bruce?

 I can't find Clark! :(

 he hasn't texted back

 something's wrong

 he's

Msg failed to send

SEND

DATE: MARCH 10

USERNAME: BWAYNE

RE: JOURNAL ENTRY 19

I'VE BEEN HOME, SUSPENDED FROM SCHOOL FOR THE PAST WEEK. NOW MY FIRST DAY BACK AND SOMETHING HAS HAPPENED TO CLARK AND DIANA. THEY'RE MISSING. THEY AREN'T ANSWERING THEIR TEXTS OR EMAILS. I'M FEARING THE WORST.

WHAT I WON'T DO IS PANIC OR QUIT. I'M SURE THOSE RESPONSIBLE EXPECT AND WANT THAT TO HAPPEN. I WON'T GIVE THEM THAT SATISFACTION.

NOW MORE THAN EVER, I NEED TO BECOME THE GREATEST INVESTIGATOR . . . THE GREATEST DETECTIVE I CAN BE.

157

DATE: MARCH 16

USERNAME: BWAYNE

RE: JOURNAL ENTRY 20

CLARK AND DIANA HAVE CHANGED AND IT'S NOT
GOOD. UNTIL I'M ABLE TO DISCOVER WHO AND WHAT
DID THIS, AND HOW TO REVERSE IT . . . I NEED
TO HIDE.

TRYING TO EVADE MY FRIENDS IS ONE OF THE HARDEST
THINGS I'VE HAD TO DO. I'VE MANAGED TO STAY OUT
OF SIGHT USING THE VENTILATION SHAFTS TO MOVE
AROUND CAMPUS. I SWEAR I HEARD CLARK SAY HE CAN
SEE THROUGH WALLS. BUT SOMEHOW HE ISN'T ABLE TO
SEE THROUGH A SIMPLE LEAD-LINED SHAFT.

WITH THE INCREASED NINJA PATROLS, IT'S ONLY A
MATTER OF TIME BEFORE I GET CAUGHT. SO I HAVE
TO THINK FAST, WEAR MY BATMAN COSTUME DISGUISE,
AND GO FIND CLUES, STARTING WITH MY FRIENDS'
LOCKERS. SEE IF THERE'S ANYTHING THERE THAT CAN
HELP ME.

HOW NOT TO CAPTURE YOUR FRIENDS:

HALLWAY-MONITOR 02

11:22:14

HALLWAY-MONITOR 03

11:31:16

HALLWAY-MONITOR 01

11:35:12

DATE: MARCH 17

USERNAME: BWAYNE

RE: JOURNAL ENTRY 21

CAPTURING MY FRIENDS PROVED TO BE TOUGH. BUT
I MANAGED TO GET THEM DOWN TO THE BASEMENT TO
QUESTION THEM. DIANA'S LASSO FROM HER LOCKER
ACTUALLY HAS SPECIAL PROPERTIES. SOME MIGHT SAY
MAGIC. BUT DEFINITELY HELPS GET TO THE TRUTH.

THEY TELL ME THAT DR. SIVANA CREATED A HELMET
ALONG WITH TECHNOLOGY FROM MR. TETCH TO MAKE THE
USER THAT WEARS IT SUSCEPTIBLE TO COMMANDS. A
BRAINWASH DEVICE! TALIA WAS ALSO AN ACCOMPLICE.
BUT THEY DON'T KNOW IF THE PRINCIPAL IS IN
CHARGE.

THIS ROPE COULD DEFINITELY COME IN HANDY LATER.
ALFRED WOULD NEVER BE ABLE TO HIDE SNACKS FROM
ME IN THE HOUSE EVER AGAIN.

WHO IS RESPONSIBLE FOR THIS SCHOOL, TALIA? FOR EVERYTHING HERE?

I CAN ANSWER. THAT WOULD BE ME.

I AM YOUR PRINCIPAL. HER FATHER. AND MY NAME IS *RĀ'S AL GHŪL!*

172

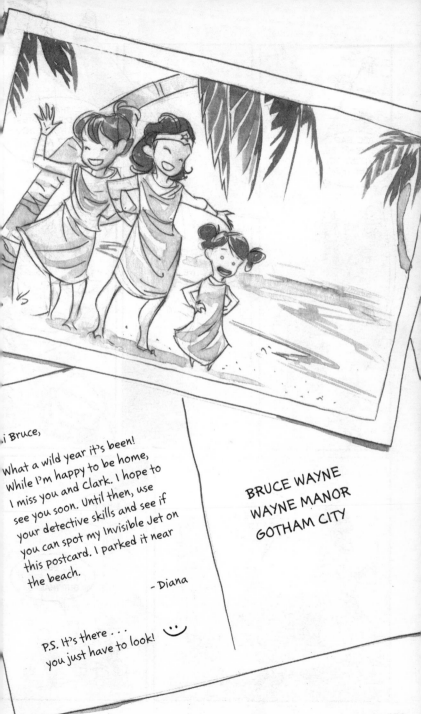

i Bruce,

What a wild year it's been!
While I'm happy to be home,
I miss you and Clark. I hope to
see you soon. Until then, use
your detective skills and see if
you can spot my Invisible Jet on
this postcard. I parked it near
the beach.

                  – Diana

BRUCE WAYNE
WAYNE MANOR
GOTHAM CITY

P.S. It's there . . .
you just have to look! ☺

DATE: MARCH 30
USERNAME: BWAYNE
RE: JOURNAL ENTRY 22

IT'S BEEN A COUPLE OF WEEKS SINCE THE DUCARD ACADEMY
SHUT DOWN FOR GOOD DUE TO OUR INVESTIGATION. THE SCHOOL
HAS EVEN BEEN REOPENED WITH PROPER EDUCATORS. WHILE
RĀ'S AL GHŪL AND HIS DAUGHTER HAVE ESCAPED, AND I
HAVE NO MEANS TO TRAVEL AND FIND NANDA PARBAT, I WILL
INSTEAD WAIT VIGILANTLY. IF THEY EVER COME BACK, I'LL
BE READY FOR THEM. THE TEACHERS INVOLVED IN THE SCANDAL
WERE ALL GIVEN COMMUNITY SERVICE AND THE STUDENTS WILL
BE SENT TO SUMMER SCHOOL. I THINK THE GOOD GUYS WON
THIS TIME.

CASE CLOSED.

I BECAME A LATE TRANSFER TO A SMALL PUBLIC SCHOOL. ONE
WHERE NOTHING WEIRD EVER HAPPENS. ONE WITHOUT NINJA OR
CLOWNS. EVEN THE CAFETERIA FOOD IS UNINSPIRING. BUT IT
BEATS THE ALTERNATIVE.

I STILL KEEP IN CONTACT WITH MY FRIENDS. CLARK WENT
BACK TO SMALLVILLE. HE'LL BE HOME TUTORED UNTIL HE CAN
START THE NEXT GRADE. DIANA IS LIVING BACK WITH HER
MOTHER AND SISTERS ON PARADISE ISLAND. THAT'S GOTTA BE
NICE!

ALFRED THINKS I SHOULD GIVE CAMP A TRY. HE SAYS IT'S
DARK IN THE FOREST. CREEPY. WITH LOTS OF BATS. AND I'
SURE A MYSTERY OR TWO TO SOLVE.

IF THERE'S ONE THING I'VE LEARNED, IT'S THAT ALFRED
ALWAYS KNOWS WHAT'S BEST FOR ME.

Case File
Folder of Rā's

[SOLVED]

Derek Fridolfs

works in the comic industry as a writer, inker, and artist on many beloved properties. With Dustin Nguyen, he co-wrote *Batman: Li'l Gotham* and *Justice League Beyond*. He's also written for such titles as *Batman: Arkham City Endgame, Arkham Unhinged, Detective Comics, Legends of the Dark Knight, Adventures of Superman, Sensation Comics Featuring Wonder Woman, Catwoman, Zatanna, JLA,* and comics based on the cartoons for *Adventure Time, Regular Show, Dexter's Laboratory, Looney Tunes,* and *Teenage Mutant Ninja Turtles*.

Derek enjoys traveling, late-night movie watching, book shopping, and just about all pizza.

This is his first children's book, and he looks forward to many more.

Dustin Nguyen

is best known for his many interpretations of Batman for DC Comics, including the co-creation of DC's all-ages series *Batman: Li'l Gotham,* written by himself and Derek Fridolfs. Currently, he illustrates lots and lots of robots and aliens on *Descender*, a monthly comic published through Image Comics, of which he is also co-creator, alongside artist/writer Jeff Lemire. Outside of comics, Dustin also moonlights as a conceptual artist for toys and consumer products, games, and animation. He enjoys sleeping, driving, and sketching things he cares about.